COMPREHENSIVE GUIDE FOR PLAB, REGISTRATION AND VISA ISSUES FOR DOCTORS BY UK PROFESSIONALS.

By

Dr Bilal Haider Malik

Tajammal Nadeem Butt

<u>Preface</u>

This is one of its kind books that provide information about the General Medical Council Registration process, PLAB exams, and Visa issues (faced by the candidates and their dependents coming to the U.K.) for the International Medical Graduates. This book is written by authors who have first-hand experience of these elements. With Brexit over the horizon, things can change, and so we aim to update this information in the second edition of our book, in light of the information provided by the GMC, UKVI, and UKBA.

Dr Bilal H Malik & Tajammal N Butt

<u>Disclaimer</u>

Any information provided in this book about GMC Registration and PLAB Examination process is referenced from GMC's official website and can be subjected to change as per GMC's discretion. Errors and omissions are expected. Kindly always refer to GMC's official website about registration and PLAB examination.

Introduction

International medical graduates have been looking forward to work and immigrate to the UK in numbers seen more than ever before. There are a lot of steps involved in the IMGs to realize their dreams. We, in this edition of our book, aim to facilitate IMGs through the provision of information about:

> Registration Process with the General Medical Council
> PLAB examinations
> Visa process Information

We have gathered this information through official websites of GMC, UKVI, and UKBA. So, this information can be subjected to change at the discretion of these agencies and organizations. Therefore, readers must understand the importance of seeking professional help and keeping UpToDate with the information available on respective official platforms.

International Medical Graduates

International Medical graduates are (1):

> ➤ nationals of countries outside the UK, European Economic Area (EEA) or Switzerland and graduated from a medical school outside of the UK

> ➤ UK nationals who have graduated from a medical school outside the UK, EEA or Switzerland.

> ➤ Do not have enforceable community rights.

General Medical Council (GMC) Registration

International Medical Graduates- Provisional Registration

Keeping in mind the above definition of IMG, IMGs must satisfy the following conditions to apply for a Provisional registration with the GMC (1):

> Passed PLAB 1 and PLAB 2 test.

(PLAB 2 should have been passed within two years before the date on which we approve your application. If your PLAB 2 were passed more than two years ago, you would be needed to provide evidence of your recent medical experience.)

> Not completed internship.

Note: Provisional registration is a must before starting Foundation year 1 Training posts.

International Medical Graduate- Full Registration

PLAB Route

Keeping in mind the above definition of IMG, IMGs must satisfy the following conditions to apply for a Full registration with the GMC via PLAB route (2):

- Passed PLAB 1 and PLAB 2 test.

(PLAB 2 should have been passed within two years before the date on which we approve your application. If your PLAB 2 were passed more than two years ago, you would be needed to provide evidence of your recent medical experience.)

- Completed internship.

GMC Approved Sponsorship

A candidate is eligible for this route, if (3):

➢ UK National or of a country outside the UK, EEA or Switzerland, graduated from a medical school outside the UK.

➢ No enforceable community rights.

And:

➢ Holds an acceptable PMQ (Primary Medical Qualification).

➢ Selected for PG training by a UK medical royal college or faculty, or by one of a small number of PG institutions or being sponsored by someone on GMC's list of approved sponsors.

➢ Have carried out medical practice for 3 out of the last 5 years, including the most recent 12 months.

Note: Academic version of the IELTS test or the OET (medicine version) is required for this route.

Find the list of Approved Sponsors on GMC's Website.

<u>The Acceptable UK or International Postgraduate Qualification</u>

A candidate is eligible for this route, if (4):

- ➢ UK National or of a country outside the UK, EEA or Switzerland, graduated from a medical school outside the UK.
- ➢ No enforceable community rights.
- ➢ Graduated from a medical school outside the United Kingdom.

And

- ➢ Hold an acceptable PMQ (Primary Medical Qualification).
- ➢ Hold an acceptable international or UK postgraduate qualification.

<u>**Table-1: UK Postgraduate Qualifications (19)**</u>

Awarding Body	Qualification
Joint Committee on Intercollegiate Examinations	Joint Surgical Colleges Fellowship Examination (JSCFE)
Royal College of Anaesthetists	Fellowship of the Royal College of Anaesthetists (FRCA) Primary FRCA examination
Royal College of Emergency Medicine	Membership of the College of Emergency Medicine (MCEM/MRCEM)
Royal College of Obstetricians and Gynaecologists	Membership of the Royal College of Obstetricians and Gynaecologists (MRCOG)
Royal College of Paediatrics and Child Health	Membership of the Royal College of Paediatrics and Child Health
Royal College of Pathologists	Fellowship of the Royal College of Pathologists (FRCPath) by examination only
Royal College of Physicians and Surgeons of Glasgow	Fellowship of the Royal College of Physicians and Surgeons of Glasgow

Awarding Body	Qualification
	(FRCS Glasg Ophthalmology)
Royal College of Physicians, London Royal College of Physicians, Edinburgh Royal College of Physicians and Surgeons of Glasgow	Membership of the Royal College of Physicians MRCP (UK)
Royal College of Psychiatrists	Membership of the Royal College of Psychiatrists (MRCPsych)
Royal College of Radiologists	Fellowship of the Royal College of Radiologists (FRCR)
Royal College of Surgeons Edinburgh	Membership of the Royal College of Surgeons of Edinburgh (MRCS Ed Ophthalmology) Fellowship of the Royal College of Surgeons of Edinburgh (FRCS Ed Ophthalmology)
Royal College of Surgeons of England Royal College of	Any of the following: • Intercollegiate Membership of the

Awarding Body	Qualification
Surgeons of Edinburgh Royal College of Physicians and Surgeons of Glasgow	Royal College of Surgeons - MRCS • Intercollegiate Membership of the Royal College of Surgeons - (MRCS (ENT)) • Collegiate Membership of the Royal College of Surgeons - (MRCS) • Fellowship of the Royal College of Surgeons - (following examination) (FRCS)

Table-2 - Overseas postgraduate qualifications (18)

Country	Awarding Body	Qualification
America	American Board of Pediatrics (ABP)	Diplomate of the American Board of Pediatrics - General Pediatrics
America	American Board of Anaesthesiology	Certificate of the American Board of Anaesthesiology
America	The American Board of Radiology	The American Board of Radiology Diagnostic radiology examination
Australia/New Zealand	Australian and New Zealand College of Anaesthetists	Fellowship of the Australian and New Zealand College of Anaesthetists
Australia/New Zealand	Royal Australasian College of Physicians	FRACP Adult medicine or evidence of three years of basic training (PREP) + achievement

Country	Awarding Body	Qualification
		of RACP written and clinical examinations OR FRACP Paediatrics or evidence of three years of basic training (PREP) + achievement of RACP written and clinical examinations
Australia/New Zealand	The Royal Australian and New Zealand College of Psychiatrists	Fellowship of The Royal Australian and New Zealand College of Psychiatrists (FRANZCP) awarded since January 2012
Australia/New Zealand	The Royal Australian and New Zealand College of Radiologists	Fellowship of The Royal Australian and New Zealand College of Radiologists (FRANZCR) (Clinical Radiology) Fellowship of The Royal Australian and

Country	Awarding Body	Qualification
		New Zealand College of Radiologists (FRANZCR) (Radiation Oncology)
Bangladesh	Bangladesh College of Physicians and Surgeons	Fellowship in Anaesthesia or Anaesthesiology awarded since July 1999
Canada	The Royal College of Physicians and Surgeons of Canada	The Royal College of Physicians and Surgeons of Canada - diagnostic radiology examination
Europe	European Academy of Anaesthesiology or European Society of Anaesthesiology	European Diploma in Anaesthesiology and Intensive Care
	European Society of	European Diploma of Intensive Care

Country	Awarding Body	Qualification
	Intensive Care Medicine (ESICM)	(EDIC) awarded since January 2015
Hong Kong	Hong Kong College of Physicians	Membership of the Hong Kong College of Physicians
Ireland	College of Anaesthetists of Ireland	Fellowship of the Faculty or the College of Anaesthetists [of the Royal College of Surgeons in Ireland[1]]
	Royal College of Physicians in Ireland	MRCP Medicine (Medicine of Childhood)
	Royal College of Surgeons in Ireland	MRCS (collegiate examination) MRSCI (intercollegiate examination) Fellowship of the Royal College of Surgeons Ireland Fellowship of the

Country	Awarding Body	Qualification
		Faculty or the College of Anaesthetists of the Royal College of Surgeons in Ireland Fellowship of the Faculty of Radiologists in Clinical Radiology of the Royal College of Surgeons in Ireland (FFR RCSI)
Malaysia	Ministry of Health	Master of Medicine (MMED) Malaysia with MRCP (UK) awarded since 1 July 2010 This must include four years of clinical experience (required to complete MMED) plus two years of training
Pakistan	College of Physicians and	FCPS Paediatrics Pakistan

Country	Awarding Body	Qualification
	Surgeons Pakistan	Fellowship in Anaesthesiology awarded since1998
Singapore	National University of Singapore	Master of Medicine (Paediatrics) Master of Medicine (Internal Medicine) including MRCP (UK)
Singapore	Joint Committee on Specialist Training Singapore	Master of Medicine (MMED) Singapore, plus MRCP (UK) awarded since 1 July 2010
South Africa	College of Anaesthetists of South Africa	Fellowship of the College of Anaesthetists of South Africa FCA (SA)
South Africa	Colleges of Medicine of South Africa	Fellowship of the College of Radiologists of SA FC Rad Diag (SA) - Diag Rad awarded after 1

Country	Awarding Body	Qualification
Sri Lanka	University of Colombo, Sri Lanka	October 2013 Doctor of Medicine or MD (Anaesthesiology) Doctor of Medicine or MD, (Obstetrics and Gynaecology) Doctor of Medicine or MD, (Paediatrics) Doctor of Medicine or MD (medicine) awarded after January 2017 Doctor of Medicine or MD (surgery) awarded after July 2017
West Africa	West African College of Physicians	Fellowship of the West African College of Physicians (Paediatrics)
West Indies	University of the West Indies	Doctor of Medicine (Anaesthesia) awarded since

Country	Awarding Body	Qualification
		September 2003 (Course title has since changed to Doctor of Medicine (Anaesthesia and Intensive care))

Entry to the Specialist or GP Registers CESR or CEGPR

If candidates are planning to join the Specialist Register or GP Register, they must apply for full registration and entry onto the Specialist Register or GP Register with a CESR or a CEGPR through the specialty (5).

Note: Information for this is available on GMC's website.

English language assessment

International English Language Testing System (IELTS)

IELTS must show (6):

- ➢ Test report number.
- ➢ The academic version of the test.
- ➢ Got a score of at least 7.0 in each testing area and an overall score of 7.5.
- ➢ Got these scores in the same test.

> Got these scores in the most recent sitting of the test.

IELTS scores are valid for two years.

If minimum scores achieved more than two years ago, English skills being kept up to date could still be evidenced by (6):

> Reference from a tutor or lecturer of a postgraduate course or from an employer who is based in a country where English is the first and native language.
> IELTS test report form number found on your IELTS certificate.

Occupational English Test (OET)

OET scores must show that you (7):

> Took the medicine version of the test.
> Got at least a grade 'B' in each testing area (speaking, listening, reading, and writing).
> Got those grades in the same test.

➢ Obtained the grades in your most recent sitting of the test.

OET grades are valid for two years.

If OET grades achieved over two years ago, then (7):

➢ Provide an OET candidate number.
➢ Reference from a tutor or lecturer of a postgraduate course or from an employer who is based in a country where English is the first and native language.

Primary Medical Qualification from an Acceptable Institution

PMQ from an acceptable institution can be considered if (8):

➢ Less than two years old when applying for registration and
➢ Was taught and examined solely in English.

Need to submit an original letter or certificate from your university or medical college that confirms (8):

> ➢ All of the course, including clinical activities, was taught and examined solely in English.

> ➢ At least 75% of any course-related clinical interaction, including personal contact with patients, their families, and other healthcare professionals, was conducted in English, i.e. without any translation support.

> ➢ The date that candidate passed their final exam.

The candidate also needs to confirm that they have never taken the academic IELTS test or the OET (medicine version) (8).

Also, if the candidate sat for his/her final exam more than two years ago, he/she will need to send original references from all his/her employers for the last two years, confirming his/her English language capability (8).

Reference from Employer

Confirmation from an employer might be accepted, if (9):

- ➤ Candidate has worked in a medical capacity for at least the past two years, in a country where English is the first and native language.

UK job offer

An offer of employment can only be accepted as evidence of a candidate's knowledge of English if it is from a UK healthcare organization (10). This organization must be a designated body (10).

Candidate should submit (10):

- ➤ A copy of the job offer letter.
- ➤ English language reference form from the doctor who appointed the candidate.

If a candidate has previously failed IELTS and OET, then it is unlikely that this evidence might be accepted (10).

PLAB 1

PLAB 1 tests the candidate's ability to apply his/her knowledge for the care of patients. Questions relate to current best practice in the UK, and equipment routinely available in UK hospitals (11). The exam covers the common, important, or acute conditions (those common in emergency departments) seen by trainees entering the second year of the Foundation Programme (F2) and the management of long-term conditions seen in primary care (11).

PLAB 1 is comprised of a written exam made up of 180 multiple choice questions, which must be answered within three hours (11). Each item starts with a short scenario, followed by a question. Candidate needs to choose the right answer out of the five possible answers given (11).

PLAB 1 Exam runs four times a year in the UK and some overseas locations. Exam places are limited and in high demand, and overseas exams are hosted by the British Council (11).

For the PLAB exam, candidates must have (11):

 ➢ An acceptable overseas primary medical qualification.
 ➢ Necessary knowledge of English; IELTS or OET.
 ➢ GMC Online account.

Resources to be used (12):

 ➢ The PLAB blueprint
 ➢ The Foundation Programme curriculum
 ➢ Good medical practice

If the candidate passes PLAB 1, he/she can immediately apply to take PLAB 2.

If a candidate fails PLAB 1, he/she can book to retake the exam provided they still meet all the requirements. Candidates can attempt the exam a maximum of four times.

If candidates have failed the exam four times, they can apply for one final attempt. They will need to demonstrate evidence of additional learning over 12 months and make an application to the GMC.

PLAB 2

PLAB 2 is an (OSCE) objective structured clinical exam (13).

It consists of 18 scenarios, each lasting eight minutes and aims to reflect real-life settings, including a mock consultation or an acute ward (13). The exam involves everything a UK trained doctor might expect to see on the first day of Foundation Year Two (F2) (13). All the questions relate to current best practices and should be answered with published evidence (13).

The PLAB blueprint sets out the scope and content of the test (13). Candidates should familiarise themselves with BNF (British National Formulary) as well.

During the exam, candidates will be marked against three areas or 'domains' for each scenario (14):

> Data gathering, technical and assessment skills

> Clinical management skills

> Interpersonal skills

PLAB 2 takes place at the clinical assessment center in Manchester, UK.

Resources to be used (14):

> The PLAB blueprint

> The Foundation Programme curriculum

> Good medical practice

When candidates pass the exam, they can apply for registration with a license to practice. They should have their application for registration with a license to practice in the UK approved within two years of passing part 2 of the exam. This applies from the point they take part 2, not the date they get their results. If they have passed PLAB part 2 more than two years ago, they will need to provide additional evidence of their knowledge and skills.

To be eligible for an additional attempt for PLAB 2 (after the fourth attempt), there must be at least 12 months between the fourth attempt and requesting an extra attempt (15). Candidates should undertake further learning to improve their medical knowledge and clinical skills (15). Candidates must have completed either 12 months' clinical practice or postgraduate qualification (15).

<u>UKMLA</u>

The UKMLA is the proposed assessment for all doctors who wish to practice medicine in the UK. This will be a requirement for all those graduating from UK medical schools from 2023, and IMG who wish to practice in the UK (17). The GMC states that the UKMLA aims to set "a common threshold for safe practice" (16).

The UKMLA will be composed of two parts (17):

- ➤ AKT (Applied Knowledge Test)
- ➤ CPSA (Clinical and Professional Skills Assessment)

AKT

The knowledge component of the UKMLA. The GMC Council approved model of the AKT will be made up of 150-200 Single Best Answer questions (17).

CPSA

The practical aspect of the exam. CPSA for international medical graduates will be carried out at the clinical assessment center in Manchester. It will be similar to the existing PLAB 2 exam.

References

1- Provisional registration for international medical graduates - GMC [Internet]. [cited 2020 Jan 7]. Available from: https://www.gmc-uk.org/registration-and-licensing/join-the-register/registration-applications/application-guides/provisional-registration-for-international-medical-graduates

2- Full registration for international medical graduates - GMC [Internet]. [cited 2020 Jan 7]. Available from: https://www.gmc-uk.org/registration-and-licensing/join-the-register/registration-applications/application-guides/full-registration-for-international-medical-graduates

3- Full registration for doctors with sponsorship - GMC [Internet]. [cited

2020 Jan 7]. Available from: https://www.gmc-uk.org/registration-and-licensing/join-the-register/registration-applications/application-guides/full-registration-for-doctors-with-sponsorship

4- Full registration for international medical graduates with a postgraduate qualification - GMC [Internet]. [cited 2020 Jan 7]. Available from: https://www.gmc-uk.org/registration-and-licensing/join-the-register/registration-applications/application-guides/full-registration-for-international-medical-graduates-with-a-postgraduate-qualification

5- CESR with registration - GMC [Internet]. [cited 2020 Jan 7]. Available from: https://www.gmc-uk.org/registration-and-licensing/join-

the-register/registration-
applications/specialist-application-
guides/cesr-with-registration

6- Using your IELTS certificate - GMC
[Internet]. [cited 2020 Jan 8].
Available from: https://www.gmc-
uk.org/registration-and-licensing/join-
the-register/before-you-
apply/evidence-of-your-knowledge-
of-english/using-your-ielts-certificate

7- Using your OET certificate - GMC
[Internet]. [cited 2020 Jan 8].
Available from: https://www.gmc-
uk.org/registration-and-licensing/join-
the-register/before-you-
apply/evidence-of-your-knowledge-
of-english/using-your-oet-certificate

8- Using your primary medical
qualification - GMC [Internet]. [cited
2020 Jan 8]. Available from:
https://www.gmc-uk.org/registration-
and-licensing/join-the-

register/before-you-apply/evidence-of-your-knowledge-of-english/using-your-primary-medical-qualification

9- Using confirmation from your employer - GMC [Internet]. [cited 2020 Jan 8]. Available from: https://www.gmc-uk.org/registration-and-licensing/join-the-register/before-you-apply/evidence-of-your-knowledge-of-english/using-confirmation-from-your-employer

10- Using your UK job offer - GMC [Internet]. [cited 2020 Jan 8]. Available from: https://www.gmc-uk.org/registration-and-licensing/join-the-register/before-you-apply/evidence-of-your-knowledge-of-english/using-your-uk-job-offer

11- What is PLAB 1 - GMC [Internet]. [cited 2020 Jan 8]. Available from: https://www.gmc-uk.org/registration-and-licensing/join-the-register/plab/plab-1-guide/what-is-plab-1

12- What resources should you use to prepare - GMC [Internet]. [cited 2020 Jan 8]. Available from: https://www.gmc-uk.org/registration-and-licensing/join-the-register/plab/plab-1-guide/what-resources-should-you-use-to-prepare

13- What is the PLAB 2 exam - GMC [Internet]. [cited 2020 Jan 8]. Available from: https://www.gmc-uk.org/registration-and-licensing/join-the-register/plab/plab-2-guide/what-is-the-plab-2-exam

14- How will you be tested - GMC [Internet]. [cited 2020 Jan 8]. Available from: https://www.gmc-uk.org/registration-and-licensing/join-the-register/plab/plab-2-guide/how-will-you-be-tested

15- Are you eligible for an additional attempt - GMC. https://www.gmc-uk.org/registration-and-licensing/join-the-register/plab/plab-2-guide/are-you-eligible-for-an-additional-attempt

16- The Medical Licensing Assessment [Internet]. Gmc-uk.org. Available from: https://www.gmc-uk.org/education/standards-guidance-and-curricula/projects/medical-licensing-assessment

17- About the Medical Licensing Assessment [Internet]. Gmc-uk.org. Available from: https://www.gmc-uk.org/education/standards-guidance-and-curricula/projects/medical-licensing -assessment/about-the-mla

18- Acceptable postgraduate qualifications - GMC [Internet]. [cited 2020 Jan 9]. Available from: https://www.gmc-uk.org/registration-and-licensing/join-the-register/before-you-apply/acceptable-postgraduate-qualifications#overseas

19- Acceptable postgraduate qualifications - GMC [Internet]. [cited 2020 Jan 9]. Available from: https://www.gmc-uk.org/registration-and-licensing/join-the-register/before-you-apply/acceptable-postgraduate-qualifications#UK

UK Settlement Route: Understanding Current Immigration Regime for Foreign Doctors wishing to work in the UK

Working for the National Health Service [NHS], United Kingdom

It may come as a little surprise for some of you that NHS is the world's largest publicly funded health service, dealing with over one million patients every 36 hours. It employs more than 1.3 million people and is heavily reliant on staff from overseas. Its annual expenditure is estimated at around £105 billion[1].

According to a careful estimate by the Office for National Statistics, around 139,000 of the 1.3 million NHS employees are foreign nationals — equating to one in eight (12.5

---

[1] https://www.ons.gov.uk

percent). Of these, around 62,000 – or 5.6 percent of all employees come from the EU countries. 45,000 come from Asia, and 21,000 are from African countries. The most common nationalities are Indian (18,300), Filipino (15,400), Irish (13,000), and Polish (8,500).

Recent official figures show that the NHS in England alone is short of 9,982 doctors. This level of shortage would leave any sane mind wondering why on earth such an amazing and gigantic service faces such shortage. The part of its answer lies in the immigration rules and policies of the UK, Home Office -UK Visas and Immigration [UKVI].

Under the current immigration system, the maximum number of non-EEA skilled workers of all different types able to come and work in the UK on a Tier-2 Point Based System [PBS] is capped at 20,700 a year – a ceiling set by the Home Office. Such visa restrictions have been a major obstacle to recruiting much-needed medical staff. For NHS hospitals, it has resulted in unfilled vacancies, often filled by paying premium locum rates.

Nevertheless, following a vociferous campaign by NHS organizations and various medical groups, the immigration rules for overseas doctors have now been relaxed. Since 06 July 2018, it has been recognized by the Home Office that medics should be taken out of the cap on skilled workers allowed to work in Britain, to help tackle the NHS's deepening workforce crisis. Accordingly, doctors and nurses are currently exempt from the annual tier-2 visa cap. Good news!

Furthermore, the Home Office has also agreed to expand the Medical Training Initiative (MTI) under the Tier 5 Government Authorised Exchange visa. The scheme would allow more medical trainees to study and work in the UK within the NHS, helping to ease staff shortages [currently put on hold by the Home Office]. Under existing rules, the government authorized program allows up to 1,000 trainee doctors from outside the EU to work in the UK for a maximum of two years. We will discuss the MTI scheme later in this book.

Immigration requirements for doctors

As you may have read through previous part of this book whereby comprehensive details have been set out about different types of professional registrations [provisional or full registration, GP or specialist registration] that non-EEA doctors require with the General Medical Council (GMC) before qualifying for permission to enter and work in the UK. Their qualification to enter and work is determined under immigration rules set by the Home Office. Once a foreign doctor has attained the relevant registration which qualifies him/her to apply for a job within NHS, there are several visa routes under which s/he can apply for a UK visa.

Unfortunately, or perhaps strangely, the UK's immigration laws regime is not as straight forward as one might think of. Not only the practicing immigration law professionals [including Solicitors/Barristers] but also the immigration judges equally disgust and criticize the complexity and obscurity of the current immigration laws. Sometimes, the complex drafting of immigration laws can be made even more difficult by populist political objectives.

UK DOMESTIC LAWS	*GUIDANCE AND POLICY DOCUMENTS*	*IMMIGRATION RULES*
1. IMMIGRATION ACT 1971 2. BRITISH NATIONALITY ACT 1981 3. IMMIGRATION AND ASYLUM ACT 1999 4. NATIONALITY, IMMIGRATION AND ASYLUM ACT 2002 5. IMMIGRATION, ASYLUM AND NATIONALITY ACT 2006 6. UK BORDERS ACT 2007 7. BORDER, CITIZENSHIP AND IMMIGRATION ACT 2009 8. IMMIGRATION ACT 2014 9. IMMIGRATION 2017	Over 600 different immigration guidance and policy documents	Over 10,000 pages of Rules covering the issuing of visas

UK Immigration Laws

The Immigration rules as introduced under the UK's first 1971 Immigration Act have grown from 40 pages to the following cumbersome volume:

Nevertheless, you don't need to worry about their dinosauric volume as luckily, the rules don't require you to have memorized or read all of them as a pre-requisite for visa grant. Anyways, we will try to make them as easy and simple as reasonably possible and without putting you to sleep:

1. Doctors who are EEA nationals

Since EEA nationals[2] have no immigration-related restrictions, the doctors who are EEA nationals have the right to work in the UK. There are certain restrictions on Croatian nationals since they may be subject to worker authorization unless they are exempt from authorization. Exemptions from the scheme are set out and found on the home office website: [https://www.gov.uk/government/organisations/uk-visas-and-immigration]

2. Doctors from non-EEA nationalities

Certain non-EEA nationals who are the spouse or partner of an EEA citizen may also have the right to enter and work in the UK. A right to entry may also be conferred by ancestry. Doctors who may have such individual rights are advised to check the Home Office website and contact them for individual or general advice.

---

[2]EEA nationals- include nationals of Austria, Belgium, Bulgaria, Croatia, Republic of Cyprus, Czech Republic, Denmark, Estonia, Finland, France, Germany, Greece, Hungary, Ireland, Italy, Latvia, Lithuania, Luxembourg, Malta, Netherlands, Poland, Portugal, Romania, Slovakia, Slovenia, Spain, Sweden, and the Unite

Unlike EEA nationals, all non-EEA nationals are subject to immigration control.

There are four tiers [Tier-1, Tier-2, Tier-3, Tier-4] within the UK's current points-based system for non-EEA national doctors to enter the UK to work, train, or study. Out of three of the relevant tiers [Tier-1, 2, and 4], Tier-2 is perhaps the most relevant and better option for overseas doctors.

We will look into and share more information about tier-2 below:

(i) - Tier 2 - General Work Visa

Tier 2 is an employer-led route within the immigration system that allows UK employers, including the NHS, to recruit individuals from outside the UK and EEA by sponsoring them to fill vacancies. The recruitment might be either to approved training or to non-training posts, provided the employer has advertised for a set period and been unable to recruit the suitable UK or EEA worker from the UK.

Health Education England[3] [HEE] is now responsible for the sponsorship of all Medical and Dental trainees for their Tier 2 visa application in England.

All doctors wishing to work in any capacity in the UK, whether in the NHS or elsewhere, must be registered and licensed to practice with the GMC[4]. It a criminal offense[5] for an employer to knowingly employ a person who requires, but lacks, immigration permission to work in that particular role. Employers will have to check and copy specific original documentation to make sure that the worker's permission is valid, and doctors and dentists will be expected to produce appropriate documentation on request.

Brief information about salient features of Tier-2 visa can be extracted from the below table:

---

[3]https://www.hee.nhs.uk
[4]https://www.gmc-uk.org/registration-and-licensing
[5]https://www.gov.uk/penalties-for-employing-illegal-workers

Tier-2 Visa Requirements	Visa entitlements	Visa Restrictions	Visa Switch
You must have:	You are allowed to:	You cannot:	You can switch from:
- Valid CoS [Certificate of sponsorship]: Offer of a skilled job from a licensed employer	- Do a second job with certain restrictions	- Get public funds	Tier 1
- Appropriate salary: minimum £30K	- Do voluntary work	- Apply for the second job until you have started working	Tier-2 Tier-4

Tier-2 Visa Requirements	Visa entitlements	Visa Restrictions	Visa Switch
		for your sponsor	
- English Language - B1 CEFR [UK Bachelor/Master's/Ph.D.]	- Study without interfering with your sponsored job		Start-up and Innovator Visa
- Maintenance funds: personal savings of £945 for 9 days, or sponsored by A-rated employer	- Bring your family [spouse or partner and children] with you		-Spouse visa
Duration of initial visa:	**Further Visa Extension of**	**Settlement after completion**	British citizenship after 6 years

Tier-2 Visa Requirements	Visa entitlements	Visa Restrictions	Visa Switch
Up to 3 years	up to 5 years	of 5 years	

In a nutshell, Tier 2 visa allows entry and stay of doctors who:

- Have been offered a job by the NHS [employer] either through complying or exemption of Resident Labour Market Test [RLMT].
- Employer will assign doctors a Certificate of sponsorship [electronic record-holding their personal information and details about the job being offered]
- Satisfy English language [B1 CEFR] and maintenance funds requirements [£945]

(a) - Resident Labour Market Test [RLMT]

Under the UK current immigration rules, most skilled jobs need to be advertised for twenty-eight days to enable UK nationals and citizens of the EU/European Economic Area (EEA) and those who already have the right to work in the UK to apply. This is called the Resident Labour Market Test [RLMT]. The purpose of RLMT is to satisfy the Home Office that vacancies are being offered first to UK or EEA nationals.

Nevertheless, the RLMT does not apply if:

- The job being offered is on the shortage occupation list*, or
- The applicant is already on Tier 2 (General) visa, or
- The job yields more than £155,300 per annum, or
- The applicant has been already working under a National Training Number (the number given to doctors when they start specialty

training) and is applying to continue a training program using the same number.

Those tier 2 trainees currently sponsored in training programs throughout England will be exempt from the Resident Labour Market Test (RLMT) and will be eligible to apply for and be offered medical and dental training posts throughout England. This will allow trainees to preference different LETB's during specialty training applications without having to consider meeting the requirements of the RLMT.

(b) - Shortage Occupation List

The shortage occupation list[6] is an official list of occupations for which there are not enough

---

[6]https://www.gov.uk/guidance/immigration-rules/immigration-rules-

resident workers to fill vacancies across the UK. Currently, there are two Tier 2 Shortage Occupation Lists:

- the UK list applies to the entire United Kingdom (including Scotland)
- the Scotland list applies only to Scotland.

It is interesting to note that Non-UK/EEA nationals who have graduated from a UK medical school will have an exemption from meeting the RLMT when moving from their Foundation Programme (in Tier 4) directly into specialty training (in Tier 2). This is a one-off exemption when switching from Tier 4 to Tier 2 visa categories.

Sponsoring non-EEA national doctors under Tier-2

In case of recruiting overseas doctors, the NHS [as Home Office Tier-2 licensed sponsor] will

---

appendix-k-shortage-occupation-list

issue a certificate of sponsorship (an electronic reference number) confirming that they have recruited that particular worker, who would use that number to apply for entry clearance to the UK. The sponsored worker will perform the job they were sponsored for. Other work cannot be undertaken, except for supplementary work in the same occupation for up to 20 hours a week outside the normal working hours of the sponsored employment, or for voluntary work. If any other new employment is sought, a new certificate of sponsorship from the new employer or sponsor will be required.

Settlement under Tier-2

First Tier-2 visa can be given for up to three years to live and work in the UK with prospects of further extension (maximum 6x yrs) provided relevant visa requirements are met. Following the completion of five years of residence in the UK under the Tier-2 visa, it is possible to apply for Indefinite Leave to Remain (ILR), also known as permanent residency.

British Citizenship

Generally, Tier-2 holders become eligible to apply for British citizenship following completion of 12 months after the grant of settlement in the UK unless they are married to a British citizen, in which case they can apply for British citizenship as soon as they become settled.

Briefly, to become naturalized, applicants are required to satisfy certain conditions under British Nationality Act 1981, more specifically - passing Life in the UK and English Language Test, good character requirements and less than 90 days' absence from the UK in the preceding year.

Dependant family members of Tier-2 visa holders

As indicated above, the dependent family members can accompany Tier-2 visa holders and will follow his/her immigration status in the UK. Usually, they will be eligible to apply for further visa extension, settlement, and naturalization at the same time as their main Tier-2 visa holder family member.

(ii) - Tier-5 Temporary Workers – Government Authorised Exchange – Medical Training initiative (MTi)

There is another exciting option available for overseas doctors to enter and train in the UK. It is set out and governed under the Tier-5 visa category of the Immigration Rules. We will try to explain and explore this option below for your ease.

This visa category is for overseas nationals coming to the UK to undertake exchanges or education and training initiatives authorized by Government departments. The Medical Training Initiative (MTI) is the scheme operated in the NHS for doctors and dentists.

MTi scheme provides various opportunities for the training and development of overseas doctors and dentists. These places are made available using capacity within the UK that is not required for UK/EEA planned training. Unlike Tier 2, employers do not sponsor these schemes. Instead, they have to be approved by the NHS locally, through local education and training boards (LETBs) or deaneries, and by the Medical Royal College for the specialty.

Further Medical Training Initiative scheme information is available on the aoMrc website [https://www.aomrc.org.uk/medical-training-initiative]

Medical Training initiative (MTi)

Visa Requirements	Duration of visa/Switching	Settlement
- **CoS from UK Tier-5 sponsor**	- up to Maximum duration of 2 years	- This visa route doesn't lead to settlement
- **Attributes - Qualification, experience as desired by Tier-5 sponsor**	- No further extension - Cant switch visa into any other visa category	- Time spent under this route will not count towards residency under any other PBS visa route
- **Funds: £945 in personal savings or guaranteed by A-rated sponsor**	- Applicants must leave the UK after 2 years and apply for a different visa route to return here	

(iii) - Other Work Visas Leading to Settlement in the UK

There are various other options open for immigrants to enter and work in the UK, depending upon their personal and familial circumstances.

- Partner or spouse visa

- UK ancestry visa

- Asylum and Human Right based applications
  are another avenue for some applicants
  based on their individual and particularly
  exceptional circumstances

These options can be explored further by
contacting the author
if needed.

www.ingramcontent.com/pod-product-compliance
Lightning Source LLC
Chambersburg PA
CBHW070317160726
47999CB00003B/1058